For the three who taught me how to be steady.

A Language Not Of Words

Written by
Mary-Kate Louis

ISBN: 978-1-7641591-3-5

Acknowledgement of Country

I acknowledge the Traditional Owners of the lands on which these poems were born. I pay my respects to Elders past and present, and I recognise their enduring connection to land, waters, and culture.

As a seeker of truth, I believe I did not write these stories alone. It has been a profound privilege to craft this poetry on this land, and I truly believe the Ancestors and Elders were with me, whispering through the wind and the wattle, guiding my hand as I found the words to tell my truth.

Sovereign union was never ceded.

A Language Not Of Words

Written by

Mary-Kate Louis

Table of Contents

ACT 1 : THE SCAR

1000
Seed
The Glass Cage
The Echo of the Bad One
Permission to be Steady

1000

I have lived a thousand different years,
yet the map upon my face remains unchanged
since the day I left that most unfamiliar place—
the only home a soul can know without fear.
Heaven is not the destination,
but the origin we carry
to learn in the heat of this hell.
I return to the start,
where love is not a feeling,
but the blueprint of our bones.
After meeting a thousand versions of ourselves,
we are finally free to return to the land
where it all began—
Us.

Seed

You called me the bottom of the barrel.
You scraped at the wood until my fingers bled,
trying to find the limit of how much a woman
could disappear.

You told the world I was a storm that needed to be
tamed,
a crazy thing with no ground beneath my feet.

But you forgot one thing about the bottom of the
barrel:
That is where the seeds are kept.
That is where the foundation begins.

You got mad because I wasn't sinking.
I was planting.
And now,

I've grown.

The Glass Cage

They built a room made of invisible walls
and told me it was for my own protection.

I could see the sky, but I could not feel the
wind.
I could see the road,
but my feet were tied to the floor of their
expectations.

They watched me through the glass,
waiting for the moment I would stop beating
my wings against the silence.

What they didn't realise is that
glass is only sand that has been under too
much heat.

And I have always known how to walk
through fire.

The Echo of The Bad One

The labels they gave me were too small to
fit the span of my heart.

Difficult. Crazy. The bad one.

I wore them like a coat that was three sizes
too tight, until the seams finally

burst under the pressure of my own truth.

Now, I leave those labels on the floor of the
house I am leaving behind.

They can keep the coat.

I am going where the air is wide enough for
me to

breathe.

Permission To Be Steady

I am held in the quiet tension
between court orders
and men who once claimed
a piece of my story.
The in-between is a heavy country.
I have no desire
to point fingers or place blame;
I am finished
carrying any version of shame.
As I watch myself
rise above the garden of hatred
they tried to sow,
I find the only question left:
Do I truly need
their permission to go? >
Or have I simply outgrown
the silence they showed
to the little people
I helped to grow?
Looking at three faces—
excited, vibrant, ready—
I realize I don't need
a signed piece of paper
to apologise
for choosing to be steady.

ACT II : THE RED EARTH

Redemption
The Parting Gift
I mourn

Redemption

I remember nights in Australia—
sometimes warm, sometimes so cold
you could feel the crisp air
cutting through your lungs.
People call it the lucky country,
but I was a stranger in my own home.
The land where I took my first breath
was the place that held my soul
only until it was ready.
I always felt a sadness
living in a place that held
the memory of theft—
where its people had no care
to repair the damage
they profited from.
It made my blood boil
until the steam met the wind
and pushed us
in a different direction.
I have an unspoken love
for the traditional owners;
I feel their pain as they reconcile
who they are and where they belong,
fighting for the right to exist

beyond glass cages
built by those who feel
nothing but victory.
Now, I am off to the origin story—
the one that came here
and tried to destroy
an entire people.
Maybe this is redemption.
When I build
what I was destined to build,
I will come back
and give my home's people
back its soul.

The Parting Gift

I am kneeling one last time

where the red dust meets the salt of the sea.

I am leaving the heat that scorched me

and the wind that carried my secrets across
the wattle.

I do not take the land with me; that would be
another theft.

Instead, I take the way the horizon taught
me how to look for what is coming.

I leave my shadow in the scrub,

a ghost of the woman who was afraid to fly.

When I land, I will be nothing but light.

I Mourn

I mourn the loss
of a culture
that isn't mine to take.

I miss learning the sounds of
Didgeridoos and clapping sticks.
I watch them dance barefoot on red soil
as if their skin were braided
into the earth—
roots older than memory,
older than the sun.

And here I stand,
speaking English
on a land that hears soul
more clearly than it hears voices.
A land whose ancestors now live in bowls,
in ashes,
in stories.

A land bequeathed to the coloniser
who mocks its people
even as he burns
in their sun.

I miss their stories—
circles of voices,
Dreaming woven into smoke—
but I stand alone
trying to reconcile the truth:
that this land remembers
the whip,
the stolen children,
the mothers who could not sit
beside the coloniser man
after he planted his seed
and took her land.

The stories miss me,
as the French say, *tu me manques*-
because I am the one
who still bends down to pray.
Pray for their children
to dance in the firelight,
and rise knowing
their survival is a legacy,
their presence a victory,
their future a land
where we live as kin,
not conqueror
and conquered.

ACT III : THE TETHER

The Digital Reach
The Unspoken
Moon x Sun
Conjunction

The Digital Reach

It's sad, isn't it?
That the people
with the biggest hearts
end up alone—
or worse,
loving the wrong people.
And here I am,
dreaming of a love
I have felt in my bones
and heard in my sleep.
My wildest dreams
are of him,
and yet I see him
on a screen—
trying to reach
for the very thing
that is —

me.

The Unspoken

I am learning
that a foundation
is not made of concrete,
but of the quiet moments
where we decide
to stay.

You are the beam
that holds the ceiling
of my dreams
just high enough
for me to stand.

We are building
a room
where the windows
look out
onto a world
we haven't
even invented
yet.

Moon x Sun

I am the Moon, cool and silvered,

orbiting a world that hasn't yet learned my name.

And you are the Sun—

a gold so fierce it burns the edges of every morning I have ever known.

I must admit the truth: I only shine because I am the reflection of you.

My light is a borrowed thing, a soft echo of your heat.

We stand at opposite ends of the sky—

a distance that should be a breaking point.

Yet, we function as one.

Without your fire, I am a stone in the dark.

Without my quiet, you would have no place for your light to rest.

Different worlds, same breath;

tethered by a gravity only the heart can recognise.

Conjunction

They say we are mirrors,
but I think we are more like a map
being drawn in real-time.

Conjunctions are when
two celestial bodies
meet at the same point
In the sky.

Every stranger I have ever met,
every hand I have held and let go,
was a compass point leading me back to the centre.

It turns out that finding you was
just a different way of finding myself.

We are the same light wearing two different faces;
a rare alignment where the "I" and
the "You" blur into a single "We."

Every person who crossed our path
was only there to polish the glass,
until the reflection became so clear
I couldn't tell where my soul ended and yours began.

ACT IV : THE FLIGHT

The Announcement

The Three Anchors

The Archive of Small Things

The Weight of the Suitcase

The Rarest Pearl

The Announcement

I had a passport,
almost expired,
with empty pages
that should have been
filled with stamps.

They would not let us go.

This time, however,
they cannot stop us.
We are not asking for permission
to leave;

we are announcing
our arrival.

The Three Anchors

You are the three small stars
I carry in my pockets
as we cross the hemisphere.
You do not ask for maps
or legal briefs;
you only ask if there will be
a park with green grass
and a sky that doesn't
remind you of the silence.
They tried to say
that moving you
was a risk,
but I look at your faces
and I see the truth:
Staying was the storm.
Leaving is the horizon.
I am building a house
of soft voices
and steady mornings,
where your laughter
is the only law
we recognise.

The Archive of Small Things

They did not pack the heavy things.
They left the wooden blocks
and the plastic trucks
that made too much noise
in the hallway.
Instead, they chose
the archives of the heart:
A single, frayed ribbon.
A drawing of a cat
with five legs.
A smooth stone
from the garden
they are not allowed
to miss.
They are teaching me
that "home"
is a light-weight thing.
It is not the roof,
or the fence,
or the signed paper—
it is whatever we can carry
in the palms
of our six
small hands.

The Weight of the Suitcase

I am packing my life
into a box made of zippers and fabric.
It smells of eucalyptus
and the dust of a room
I will never sleep in again.
People ask me
what the air will be like
on the other side.
Will it smell of damp stone?
Of ancient rain?
Of a thousand years
of people rushing
to find their own "home"?
I don't tell them
that I don't know.
I only know
that the air here
has become too thin
to hold my dreams,
and I am willing
to fly until I find
an atmosphere
heavy enough
for me to finally
land.

The Rarest Pearl

I stepped off a plane thinking I was crazy—
following a thread that made me hazy.
My life turned upside down and inside out;
a love so great it made me shout
across a tether no one could see.
But here I was, across the world,
trying to find the rarest pearl.

ACT V : THE SOVEREIGN

The Precipice

The Touchdown

The First Morning

The New Metric

The Printing Press

The Precipice

He told his friends and family she was crazy;
he saw their faces swallowed by pity,
and sighed with relief
that he had convinced the world
she was the bad one.

But now, as they linger on the pages
of books where her name is printed,
where her face is plastered
and her story told—
are they confused?
As to why
this bottom-of-the-barrel woman
managed to surpass her victims
in success, in motherhood, in soul?
Or do they cling to the idea
that she is a manipulator?

The smartest manipulator to fool the world...
As she stands at the precipice of greatness,
she wonders:
Why do you still care?

The Touchdown

The wheels meet the tarmac
with a kiss
that says: You are here.

Eight hands
reach for the seatbelts,
six eyes
look out at a sky
that doesn't know
our secrets.

We are not
the "bad ones"
Here.

We are just
a family
starting
at the beginning
of the light.

The First Morning

The light in London
is a different kind
of silver.
It doesn't roar
like the sun
I used to know;
it whispers.
It catches
the steam of my coffee
and the way
you look
before the world
starts to move.
I am a stranger
to these streets,
but I am
no longer
a stranger
to myself.
Here,
in the quiet
of a new kitchen,
I am finally
learning
how to exhale.

The New Metric

I no longer measure
my worth
by the volume
of their shouting.
I measure it
by the depth
of my children's
sleep.

The Printing Press

They tried to write
my epitaph
in the dirt.
I chose
to write
my legacy
in ink.

www.ingramcontent.com/pod-product-compliance
Lightning Source LLC
LaVergne TN
LVHW051020080826
845145LV00009B/2725